Tomorrow We May Walk On Clouds

Also by Wendell Watt and published by Ginninderra Press
Oranges Grown On Trees (Picaro Poets)

Wendell Watt

Tomorrow We May Walk On Clouds

Tomorrow We May Walk On Clouds
ISBN 978 1 76109 652 5
Copyright © text Wendell Watt 2023
Cover image: Kirstin Sercombe

First published 2023 by
GINNINDERRA PRESS
PO Box 3461 Port Adelaide 5015
www.ginninderrapress.com.au

Contents

Beginnings
- Birth   9
- As the Baby Sees   11
- A Tadpole or a Fish?   12

Family
- Mudlarks   15
- Memo to Mothers   16
- Mr Merman's Pool   18
- Love and Madame Butterfly   20
- Dear Alf   21
- A Man of Opinion   22

Today
- Hi, World   27
- Red Lights   29
- Song of the Supermarket Trolley   30
- Lament of the Waiting Room Chair   32
- Get Grandpa a Cup of Tea   34
- Writers' Meeting in the Time of Coronavirus   36
- Toilet Paper   37
- Bah, Humbug   38
- Anywhere Else   39
- A Note to My Gaoler   40
- The Unconquered   42
- Who Are You?   43
- A Taxi Home   45
- If I Can   46
- This is History   47

Country
- Belonging   51

Jacarandas	53
A Magpie, Two White Cockatoos and I	54
A Golden Wedding	55
After Rain	56
Drought	57
Fire	58
A Necessary Thing	59
Freedom, is it?	60

Yesterday

A Virgin Land	65
Trojan Horses	67
The Eyes of the Blind	68
Look, this is all it is	70
A Postman's Job	73
Currencies	75
Travel Guide	77

Tomorrow

Countdown	81
Just For Today	82
I Am Emperor	83
We Know That	84
Tomorrow We May Walk On Clouds	85

Endings

Quicksilver Girl	89
One Dove	91
Desert Song	92
The Old Cemetery	93
The Butterfly in the Room	95
One Moment Longer	97
Who'd Want?	98

Beginnings

Birth

They snatch me, slap my cheeks, demand that I breathe.
I wait on the moment's pause. Do I breathe or not; do I stay, or go?
See me dazed by light, by forceful hands
by too many faces too close too urgent too loud.

If you stay, child, there will be
  sound:
>Whispers and shouts.
>Bells tolling, thump of drums.
>Carols in candlelit cathedrals.

  smell:
>Skin. Milk.
>Roast dinners. Old books.
>Lilies.

  sight:
>Colour. Shapes.
>Ballet elegance of trees.
>Flash-dashes of a lorikeet in grevilleas.

  touch:
>Cold. Hot.
>The outwardness of grit, of ice.
>The inwardness of love.

  language:
>Names. Meanings.
>Conversations warm as clasped hands.
>Reprimands sharp enough to cut tongues.

  friendship:
>Belonging. Honesty.
>Calm voices on stormy mornings.
>Laughter anytime.

war and peace:
> Broken hearts, hearts mended.
> Bodies cheap for killing.
> Fortunes spent for healing.

cities:
> Ambition. Affluence.
> Celebration, desperation.
> Ideas, confidence.

dying:
> Regret for things done and not done.
> Thankfulness for the story lived
> For the people known, befriended, trusted, loved.

The choice is yours. Will you stay or go?

If there were choice, who would not choose to stay?

As the Baby Sees

Granted there is joy.
Granted there is grief
also some of nothing-much-at-all.
Granted that devils wield sharp knives
that goodness has soft flesh
neutrality a thick skin;
that spilt blood is a curse
forgiveness a benediction
that there is love
if you're lucky.

It's a puzzle, a patchwork
a randomness.
It is what living is
but

see it as the baby sees:
the miracles
of flowers
clouds
leaves, bees
birds, butterflies…
The wonder.

A Tadpole or a Fish?

after a heated discussion on either possibility

I'm sure this is a tadpole not a fish.
Believe me when I say we have our wish
and that we do not need to search again.
It's pretty clear that this one is amphibian.
He'll sprout two legs to hop from place to place.
He'll grow two lungs and – yes! – a handsome face
and voice that croaks with operatic vigour.
He'll cut (to all his friends) a handsome figure.
A tadpole, as we know, is far superior
to fish who are, in every way, inferior.

Please, creature that I snatched from watery bog,
Do prove me right and grow into a frog.

Family

Mudlarks

The morning weeps
inconsolably.
Is it some hurt by ancient gods
or test
that causes such an avalanche of tears
to rain on parkland, tents, the portaloos, the stage?

The news spreads fast.
Media heave cameras through sheets of water.
Splendour in the Grass
the outdoor festival of song
a convocation of joyful youth
now changed to Splendour in the Mud.
Does the audience turn grey, and dull, and go home?
See them

buy gumboots
slosh happily through glug
release bogged cars from captivity
sleep under drips in leaky tents
roll in mud for fun
dance jump and sing along
lost in the moments and the music.
Making memories.
Declaring with pride
'I will never forget this
as long as I live.'

Still the rain comes down
while drought and fire seem only two breaths back
and the young grow stronger.

Memo to Mothers

The father is a little stout, a little grey.
Yes; he will hand her over, this daughter veiled in white
to the fellow there of whom he, more or less, approves
though no one really could be good enough.
Thus she is given to the man she loves
while doves of joy coo sweet inside her heart;
taking the ring, vowing the vows
as the priest intones with thund'rous threat
'As long as you both shall live.'
The mother sits unregarded.
Hard seat. Legs crossed. Her shoes are tight.
Officially it's nothing to do with her, this passing over of property.
Some ancient rituals die hard
but she is allowed a tear or two.

The wedding feast is generous
the bridegroom's father's speech effusive.
So pleased to welcome *(newly branded)* Mrs Scott into the family.
It's our daughter they are corralling.
Bride's choice, it was, to take their name.
Love is a devotee of new allegiances.

Mum claps and smiles
trapped by unprompted thoughts.
This daughter is ours
from the first delight of two cells darkly met.
She peels back memory and miracles.
One truly mine.
Grown in my body,
loved before knowledge,
adored before sight
embraced before touch.
Born needed, needy.
Mine.

This woman, fully made
is taken up by others now, and welcomed even
(although I would not have it otherwise).
My daughter follows the very path I trod.
How did my mother feel?
How do all mothers feel?
Bereft, like me?

Mr Merman's Pool

Oh yes, I remember
a day just like today
the sky, you could sail up and float in the blue of it
then sail down and float in its image in water
a day such as this, full-lipped
sun-driven, sleepy-eyed
while you small girl watched, dazzled,
the rainbows of sea spray fly into air and fall.

You met the merman here. Saw him sitting
on a rock beside the small sea pool, leaning
dreaming over the water
of the still small pool.
You asked, 'Are you a merman?'
He straightened up; put a finger to his lips.
'Our secret, eh?'
'But where is your tail?'
'In my sea cave home.
'I put on my legs when I visit land.'

He showed you treasures of the sea
in the still small pool: sea urchins
starfish, necklaces of seaweed
a world in still jade water
not a metre across
not half a metre deep.
'This is a pool world.
'I live in the ocean world. And you –
'You live in the land world.
'So many magic places,' he said.
Delight flared in her eyes.

Oh yes, I remember that day
full-lipped, sun-driven
and you, our daughter, bewitched by discovery.
You left us soon after.
Love failed to hold you, failed
to bring wellness back.
Through fevers you whispered
'Mr Merman's pool…'
your eyes clearing
momentarily bright
as the snatch of the sea spray's flight.
In the end he and we could delay you no longer.
I know you took Merman's hand as you were leaving us.
He would see that you entered that infinite other world gently
without fear.

You never knew that he was just a lad with seaweed in his hair.

Love and Madame Butterfly

Throughout the night
as stars turn
to celestial music
Madame Butterfly waits
for Pinkerton.
He comes
at dawn and with another woman.
'I'll take our son,' he says to Butterfly.
'You understand it's for the best.'

The opera audience boos at curtain call.
We hated him
for leaving gentle Butterfly
and turning to the safety
of a wife like himself
one whom he could take to meet his family, his friends
without a tedious explanation;
one who talked the talk, shared the history
sang the songs
and honoured the national flag with her hand upon her heart.

Do not blame him for escaping the exquisite foreign butterfly
who offended her religion, culture and her family
for love of him, which shone as sharp and bright
as sword blades
and as terrifying.
How could he look at that
without being blinded by the light of it?

Dear Alf

Sleek sleepy monster,
in sharkly contemplation
describing eternal circles with your aquarium friends.
I stare at you through glass,
not used to seeing such an instrument of death
so close and handy.
What would happen if I pushed him in?
You sleek bored monster, belly's tight, and yet
I bet you'd wake up fast and gulp him down, my loving Alf.
His flesh is tender from the armchair years
of beer and TV cricket
and lying on the grass instead of cutting it,
from sleep and sex and other wifely ministrations.
You'd snap him up, two bites, and he'd be gone,
old spongy Alf.
Instant disposal.
At least the act would be an affirmation
that even I can make things move.
But, once you got him, monster,
who then would be left for me to love?

A Man of Opinion

The stranger walking in a suburban street
past houses crouched, hatted
blinking at each other across the bitumen
is a man of opinion
who knows at a glance
that this street is a place of dead hearts
and dead ends

such as, he frowns, 'that house':
red brick, grey lawn
rosebush by the gate.
Imagines a 9 to 5 husband with dull job
the part-time wife.
Children. Brats probably.
TV and computers turned on. Off buttons forgotten
or lost.

'That house' is my house.
The one with the tired lawn
garden neglected
except for the roses tranquil with fullness
collecting sun and bees
red roses for love for my wife, ill
but fighting.
Their fragrance lights her drugged sleep.
The children look on, hold her hands
while the house, one storey, brick, six decades old
inspiration of a no-nonsense builder
becomes so filled with love
it might float away on angels' wings to Heaven.

The man cuddles his opinion
against an easy heart
and walks on.

Today

Hi, World

Let's go
rushing to Russia
careering to Korea
singing in Singapore
cancanning in Canada
galloping to the Galapagos
tying knots in Taiwan
parading in Paraguay
roaming in Romania
queuing in Cuba
running in Iran
wanting more in Morocco.

Let's be
silly in Syria
chilly in Chile
bold in Bolivia
merry in America
solemn in the Solomons
naughty in Norway
hungry in Hungary
brazen in Brazil
frank in France.

You go to Yugoslavia
I'll go to Goa
We'll catch up in Saskatchewan.

Ask why in Hawaii
finish in Finland
pack up in Pakistan
and then
stray to Australia
and home.

Red Lights

Grit is a cat-o'-nine tails
whipping across gutters
into the trunks of captured paperbarks
who should be eyeing their own reflections in a river
instead of bearing the brunt of daily floggings
by the slipstreams of passing cars.

Lights go red.
Traffic stops.
Lights stay locked
on red.

Earth rises from bruised knees
stretches, cracks bitumen.
Surprised birds sing.
Paperbarks in calm air
reach tall again.
Quiet thoughts, like spring seeds waking
stir.

Song of the Supermarket Trolley

I wait in the trolley line
hoping my turn will come
soon.

Now I feel the laying-on of hands.
A jerk.
Hurrah!
We're off
on the adventure of the aisles.

A passing smile to the plums
complacent, juicy
ready to be chosen
taken home and treasured
(they don't know they'll be eaten).
Down past the lettuce
crimped and crisped
the nuts all packaged up
away from human hands
no bulk buys any more.

She backs and turns.
Thinks I'm a camel.
Loads me with stuff.
You should be drinking tap water
ma'am.
Not bottled.
And hold on!
Bread!
What's wrong with sourdough?
Or rye?

Chats at the check-out
with trolley mates
then back to the rank
in line again
excursion ended.
Sigh.

Waiting for another laying-on of hands.

Lament of the Waiting Room Chair

I stand empty, temporarily
not pouched but padded modestly
angled average to accommodate the shape
of whoever chooses me to sit on.

It's a lottery, you know.
These people come and go; they use me once
or twice or not again.
Some grump squats on my belly
snorts with impatience
(he should know that doctors overbook)
a worrier fidgets at my willingness
with restlessness.
Words fall, like strung beads broken;
heft only happens behind closed doors
after a name is called
and my sitter stands, relieved from the tedium of me
to face the doctor, the verdict
sentence or reprieve.

I have never known
the stretch and slump of an intimate who cares
someone who finds me every day a comforter
whose body I learn and curve into my own
whose tiredness and strain I tease away
whose touch quickens a ready heart.
That would be love, you know.

Through the comings and the goings
the not-enoughness of acquaintance
I wish
to find a home where I belong.

Get Grandpa a Cup of Tea

A little snail in a hungry mood
set off one day in search of food.
Crawl
He'd nothing in his rumbling tum,
Crawl
because the fierce mid-summer sun
Crawl
had shrivelled up the plants with heat,
   Crawl
and left him not a thing to eat.
Crawl
He dreamed of juicy leaves and such.
   Crawl
He didn't want to wish for much,
Crawl
for greedy snails could sometimes burst.
   Crawl
(of burst or starving, burst was worse.)

The ground was bare. 'There's nothing here,'
he cried, and shed a worried tear.
Bee flew up smiling. 'Snail, g'day.
I met you only yesterday.
You gave me quite a friendly Hi,
when I was feeling rather shy,
and so I'd like to help you now.
Just follow me.' He made a bow,
then bizz-buzzed gently to the right.

Snail followed fast with all his might.
   Crawl
The fast of snail is pretty slow.
    Crawl
The might of snail is pretty low.
      Crawl
But put together bit by bit,
        Crawl
the slow and low make quite a hit,
         Crawl
and add to those the help of bee
          Crawl
assisting snail so friendly,
           Crawl
the little snail soon reached a plot
            Stop
of Grandpa's plants
            and ate the lot.

Writers' Meeting in the Time of Coronavirus

They cancel here, they cancel there
they cancel almost everywhere
but surely, though, the brain goes on
unstoppable as words flow on
to thoughts that have a right to be
enshrined in tales and poetry.

Our chairman John maintains his place
in poetry's so sweet embrace.
He says 'We cannot stop to play
must make the most of everyday
before the genius of our craft
sails off on someone else's raft.'

So here we come, with honour true
to Zoom together, me and you
and join our thoughts for greater things.
Thus may we wordsmiths spread our wings
and fly to heights as yet unhinted
where fulsome words spill newly minted.

Toilet Paper

Toilet paper, useful stuff.
Once we used it without thought
now in days of covid fear
searches for it come to naught.

On the beaches, on the hills
in the town and in the city
vigilantes guard their rolls
not a single grain of pity.

What's the worry? Different ways in
harder times have long been known:
use old phone books, magazines
leaves and grass that's freshly mown

left hand good for easy use.
Keep the right one clean for eating.
Careful when you meet a friend.
Clean hands are the ones for greeting.

Be creative, don't surrender.
No one needs to rob a store.
By the way, I've always wondered –
tell me, what's a bidet for?

Bah, Humbug

The trouble is
the new year doesn't know it's new.
Earth moves around the sun
time after time after time after time…
revolution after revolution after revolution…
never changes.
Then someone says, one midnight
'It's new, the year.
Now!'
They let off raves of fireworks
cheer
drink champagne
and hug
thinking their celebrations
the chemical dazzle of their lights
are special
when all they need to do
is look at the sun
rising
setting
creating painter's palette skies
for free
every single day.

New Year is special?
Bah, humbug!

Anywhere Else

They lived here, laughed here, loved here
grew angry, sad
happy
woke early
worked hard
drank strong coffee, weak tea
shared food, friendship
strength.

After the bombs and the shells
their homes gape wide to the moon.
Broken walls refuse to kneel
but supplicate lost gods
and point
defying cranky gravity
to Heaven.
Rooms sheeted by dust and rubble
house only by the ghosts of those who lived here
laughed here, loved here
and now flee
lost
to anywhere else.

A Note to My Gaoler

I am a prisoner
caught in the tide of sad centuries
locked between aching walls
punished for the evil of a new idea.
Before you return to my cell
hard with intolerance
I have a favour to ask.
Think of it as a right
not an impertinence.
Please.

Take a breather from your day job.
Create a symphony, write a poem, dig a garden
Listen to the flutes of wind and water
watch birds in flight.
Bring back to my cell
to the darkness
the silence
a memory of sun
a soft voice.

After all, my friend, we are brothers.
Our forebears' deeds
their godliness, their guilt
are printed in our body cells.

We both are vessels for fragility
and strength
for whispers, for shouting
for delight, puzzlement
and pain.

We can leap
or fall.
We can stand proud
or stand stripped.

I wait in my cell for you
colder than cold
remembering sunshine.
Some brothers are blessed by goodness.
Some cursed with cruelty.

Your choice.

The Unconquered

Dance, the devil orders. Dance.
The leering fellow with a gun aims to humiliate
wants a laugh
wants to see this feeble creature fall.

I dance. He thinks for him.
Fool. I do this for myself.

On shaky legs, strength comes.
My feet move with ancient rhythms
away from the devil's habitat
the now of threadbare days
humbling submissions, splintering of hope

to a truth where beds are soft
sleep deep, soup thick
laughter kind, respect a given.

You watch, poor devil
satisfied I know my place.
You do not understand
my dance is a temple
to the moments of grace where hope returns.

Who Are You?

Who are you?
knocking late on our door
after windows have been closed
the curtains drawn, the heater on
the television going
in the room where we sit with family
and friends
united in language and in laughter.

Who are you?
knocking on our door,
your skin so different so dark
your wife beside you and the child,
too wild, too tattered, too desperate
too hurt
to understand our complacency.
You were the hunted who escaped.
Now you ask us for kindness.
You can tell us tales that we
might not want to hear.
You trail the hot breath of bombs
and the sounds, too loud
of their exploding.
Your faces are freshly washed
but still there are bloodstains
on your clothes
and the smell of fear.

Who are you?
You feel and see as I do
and although my eyes have never seen
what yours have seen
my courage has never been tested
as yours has been
my love for family never been measured like yours
my home never been sacrificed
You are me.

A Taxi Home

A taxi home. The driving skilled.
The driver dark-skinned
from Somalia.
He has his job, a wife
two children but
'It's hard,' he says.

Money
his parents in Somalia
are needing always, asking
yesterday…today…tomorrow.
They know
their son lives in a honeyed land
where gold and food are there for taking.
Back home they're hungry,
fleeing from guns and hate
and trust their son
in the land whose streets are paved
with gold, they think.

The truth: these streets are paved with dirt and toil and hope,
and hope is a fragile thing.
My driver sighs.
'It's hard,' he says
then squares his shoulders
shakes his head
and smiles.

If I Can

If I were to tell you I am become the new Don Quixote
what would you say?

If I were to tell you I have taken up
my lance and ridden out
to conquer evil things with the courage of an honest man
would you believe me?

There is one who used a fist
on gentle evenings meant for love
one who broke a small child's innocence
and one who rooted out an old tree's pride.
Another bruised a blue and yielding sky
one breathed a town
to dust and bone
one gunned an angel
down in flight and one
stole water.

Instead of sharp swords I dream of soft words
instead of tears, of peace
but first the battle.
Someone has to do it.

The Spanish Don, they say, was insane.
No matter whether I am sane or not
if it takes a crazy man to break the devil's sorceries
someone has to do it
has to set the world to rights.
Trust me.
If I can.

This is History

This is history:
the slow bite of time
that chews up the flesh of mountains
gulps oceans whole and spits them out again
sucks rivers dry leaving fish aghast and shocked birds
   mewling
turns tree to cinder
seed to tree
tilts sand against the drought-dry bones of earth
clothes damp soil with forest
turns certainty to ash
then kindles certainty again.

This is history:
the needy surges of nations
a race displaced
the sighs of its stories faded
a language rooted out
a new one planted
old secrets revealed
old wars ended
new wars begun
hates turned to dust
new hates unmined
loves banished
loves allowed.

This is today.
Sun out. Blue sky.
Forget history.

Country

Belonging

You find colour here so pure your eyes sting in the heat of it –
a blue that sings high Cs through the slow circumference of sky
the rusty earth voracious in its joy of red
white for the marbled trunks of trees
the misted grey of saltbush leaves
the gold of spinifex reshaping, shifting, cowed by wind.

Look down. Look close
at globes of puffball seeds
at tiny honey-heavy flowers
the traceries of creepers crouched to earth
the busyness of tracks in sand –
a dingo pad
the scratch of bent stems weathervaned by air
the triplet prints of birds.

Listen.
Hear silence deep as ancient dreams veined with the urgent
    itch of life.

You straighten tall, upright above the spinifex
acacias at your chest, the hug-earth creepers at your feet.
You move in counterpoint to bush and leaves and the lizard's slur
and the brisk staccato of birds.
Your heart beats sound above the wind's soft blur.
You whisper and your voice is cupped in tiny springs.
You sing and the sand hills hum reply.

For you, grevilleas hold lit candles, mallees kneel.
A desert oak lifts arms in benediction.

Look down. Lean close. Run fingers through soft red earth.
Bend to this country known beyond knowledge, reached past
 journeying.
Learn this land as the land is learning you
and understand what belonging means.

Jacarandas

A froth, a riot
an extravagant exuberance of blue.
What show-offs they are
those jacaranda trees
needing to prove they are more beautiful
than anything else
in November streets.
They blanket the burn of flame trees
insisting 'It's our turn now'
while thumbing their noses at Christmas bush
which lights up in December.
And then, the party over
when they are done with admiration
they carpet our dirty paths with blue.

We look down
and see the blue turn into mush.
Sweep it away
thinking of next November…

A Magpie, Two White Cockatoos and I

sit on a bench.
Not much is said.
Silence is speech enough.

Cockies can be bullies, I know.
I've seen them at it
with snap and push;
magpies too can be pushy
though not as loud
but today we sit together
reflective, the wild ones and I
considering many things:
drought, fire, flood
disease.

The birds know they and I
have common cause.
We share no language.
No words are needed.
In quiet communion
we ponder life's perplexities.

A Golden Wedding

Proud to the sky
the palm tree heavy with fruitfulness
unclasps a filigree of stem and seed
that spills like a gold veil
for a gold bride
into the flare of morning sunshine.

A magpie watches the spangled seeds
dance giddy with light
in time to the soft wind's urging.
He looks not for pleasure.
The promise is all.

Suited up
formal in black and white
preening himself
he eyes the ripening crop
licks his beak
and waits for the wedding feast.

After Rain

Grass drinks, grows green, luscious.
Children now old and creaky in winter limbs
will remember how they rolled and played
small voices fluting with happiness
on the grass through summer mornings
in the springtime of their lives.

Hours drowse with humidity.
Bees flop, nectar-laden
on flowers.
Creeks run merry over rocks.
Dragonflies fold wings
and hide.

We sleep the afternoon away.
Water drips from the tap in the garden.
No one cares.

Drought

Sun sucks up moisture
tracks the sky
relentless.
Trees open arms and hands for rain
leaves turn sideways to light.
Creeks' songs are stilled.
Grass dies, crackling.
Children grizzle.

Fire

We sit in the bubble of firelight.
Warmth leaks into the cold caves of our bodies.
Watching the spit of flame and spark
the fire's shifting face
you could say we worship it.
The day has been long
we hunted and killed
now is the time for resting and feasting.
The juice of cooked meat dribbles from our fingers.

In those lost dark ages we were one, the fire and us
but knew it had the devil's temper.
Today we moderns still fear fire's anger
the dialogues with wind
the roaring, like surf surge, down valley
up mountain while skies turn red
and hell is envious.

We fight it, flee from it
yield to its majesty.

A Necessary Thing

It's the force you feel but cannot see.
A moody thing
of ups and downs
strong as a drunken punch
feathery as a baby's kiss.
Can tiptoe, skitter, skirl.
Moves leaves, houses.

It's the stroking with a cool
invisible hand
the blanketing with heat
a squeezing that pushes
milk bottles in
puffs up a plastic bag before sealing.
Supports planes and birds
holds up a column of mercury or a car
inflates tyres.
Bends light
paints sunrise, sunset, rainbows
likes blue best.
Acts handmaid to the capricious chemistry
of fire.

It's the coming up from underwater into overwater
to the magical, life-giving necessary
air.

Freedom, is it?

Tumbling, tumbling up,
I laugh at Newton and his apple falling
down
for I am breaking all the rules and tumbling
up
past cliffs of dressed stone and gargoyles ugly enough
to push the devils back but see
they are losing their leers as the city erodes their magic.
Now, as seasons shift and turn, anything goes.

I tumble up
past steeps of glass brilliant as goodness
where figures inside peering at me outside passing
know that anything goes
but believe there is a certain line that must be toed.
Inside they hand memory over to computers
have intimate relationships with screens
understand the value of a coin or two
and get what can be got with networking and paper bags
accepting that anything goes but
only so far, no further.

It shocks, this nose-thumb at gravity and accepted circumstance
those trapped ones see when inside
looking outside at me
tumbling up escaping
the jitter and confusion of a planet
where goodness fades and innocence despairs.

Tumbling up through blue sky
to darkness.
No sound of bell or bird
no conversation, laughter
no one absolutely else.

Me insignificant
in space.
Freedom, is it?

See me bending to the rules again
and turning
tumbling
home.

Yesterday

A Virgin Land

No poets, these mariners
but practical men
whose signposts are time and stars.
Opposing earth's sombre spin
their ship follows the sun
to find a land waiting to be measured
occupied and plundered.

Sailing north along the unknown coast
they survey
mark maps to pin down the edge of a continent

watch columns of smoke
unravel on shore
as fires keep pace with their white-winged ship
fires to inform
or warn others?

Which others?
Who lights the fires; who reads the smoke?
The mariners see no walls, no buildings
no cities, no ports
no townsfolk or labourers
only knotted trees, pale cliffs, white beaches
peopled by the shadows of elusive ghosts.

Who owns the purpose
the intent
the authority
to build fires of warning or welcome
in this virgin land?
The ghosts?

No matter.
The planted flag is all.

Trojan Horses

26 January 1788

Out in the ocean's emptiness
shadows press fingerprints in mist.
Moving coastwards
the shadows become boats rising
out of the sea on this summer morning
aiming straight for the harbour mouth
into the sun and still water
snug between cliff and cove
into the lives of the people
who own this land of the south
and are owned by it
who know its stars and its stories
its pleasures and its dry bones
who in awe see dreams come floating on vibrant water
like gifts of the ocean
like spirits.

Out of the mist and the sea
these boats
these Trojan horses
come.

The Eyes of the Blind

We could die
seeking destiny in this place
where the sky howls against the wind
the sun holds us in a fist of fire
and the stars cry at our desolation.

Needing water
we stumble over stone
stir dust.
Our bodies are dry leaves
dying

until God sees
and leads us to a hollow cupped by rock
filled with our lives, with water.

Why are those dark ones lined on the ridge above
ten of them, painted bizarrely, spears to hand
stamping and threatening?
What right have they to hector us
who've come to civilise this emptiness
nourish it, grow crops
produce fine wool, fat stock?
We see men tall on fruitful acres
smell roses
hear children yet unborn at play
and the lullabies of mothers.

Those dark ones pass
leaving no trails, making no marks.
Building nothing, existing barely.
They should be thanking us
instead of hurling threats above this spring
whose water reflects the eye
of our merciful God in this merciless place.
Shoot them and be done with it.

The country cries
'When shall the eyes of the blind be opened?'

Look, this is all it is

The continent is a maiden waiting.
I will split her up the middle, ease out the marrow from her bones tease out her secrets.

I am an ancient land, millennia wise, and like no other. Maiden? No!!
A warrior, more like. My skin is armour, tight-lipped. It bleeds red as rust, secretive as blood.

I will collect the secrets, write them in books, draw them in charts, tell everyone: Look, this is all it is. Tameable for those with will enough and who think it is worth their time. If nothing else, my journey will bring me fame. Men will bow. Women will hover and flutter ready eyes.

My skies are hollow with silence threaded by the complaints of wind. Sands shift. Colour shrieks. Sun shocks. You think me easy?

Lakes or oceans tremble on the horizon. No closer. Never closer.

Mirage. The devil's curse. The pot of gold that can break any man's will. A lake, only of light. A joke I play on the arrogant. When I feel like it.
Truth is I hold water like jewels in the hollows of a capricious heart.

This desert is generous with water. Or we are lucky – or brave enough because of course we are Englishmen.

This desert is also generous with heat.

It is heat that sucks the life from the living and desiccates the dead.

Heat is my big gun, my cannon, an obvious defence. I can also be more subtle than that.

Stony deserts are paved with grief. The spinifex's gold hides edges sharp as pain.

My secrets and my stories are decipherable only by my friends, the dark-skinned people who have danced with me while I have aged and shifted and stretched old bones.

The natives greet us, offer food and women. We bat these dark-skinned irritants away like flies. We want obeisance, not equality.

The wind rides me, heaves sand about, remembers the sea and fashions waves.

We surf sand hills slippery with dryness, wave upon wave that crest the curve of the earth and never break.

I sing a new song and throw a wall of jagged rock across the plains. Cutting edges, loose and piercing stones.

Minds are geared to our goal. Bodies drag on behind. Minds force air to part, earth to smooth. Remember the goal, the coast, the sea. Soon.

The northern tropic air is water suspended. Its burden will be shaken off as rain. Soon.

The ocean sends salt outriders into air and water. The earth is a sponge of liquid mud. Rain liquefies the air. The ocean, soon.

I am the crocodile in the muddy swamp, surveying invaders with patient lifted eyes. Enjoying the game.

Revelation and disappointment have made up our coming. The ocean's tidal water swells and sways in the stream where we camp but the ocean is modest and shuts itself away. It is close enough. We can say for sure that we have crossed the continent. At a price. Now there is the returning. Time is the enemy for men must eat and our food supplies are finite. So weary, eager juices drained away, we are broken by this land.

I have lured them with water and thrown all I have at them: humidity, mud, mosquitoes, wind, rain, dust, dryness, heat. And I watch them squirm.

A camel dies. We eat it.
A horse dies. We eat it.
And now?
We want to stop and stay and sleep. To bow and surrender to this maiden continent who has done us wrong. But home is south, and the cheers. Home is everything, so we cannot stop and stay and sleep. We move on and are left with nothing, no clothes, no food. Only nardoo which makes us ill. And water. And what we like to call our courage.
Must keep the Aborigines at bay. We must. Still they hover.
There is no one here to help us.
Where have we gone wrong?

In 1860-61, Burke and Wills, King and Grey were the first Europeans to cross Australia from south to north. All died on the return journey except King, who survived by accepting the help of the Aborigines.

A Postman's Job

'Biddy.' He greets her by the gate; raises his hat.
She opens the latch, smooths her hair.
Her hands are seamy creek beds full of doing.
'Mornin' Blue,' she says. His hair is grey now; still the name
    has stuck.
Patting his horse, dismounting
he extends an arm and proffers one official envelope.
There are no words for this,
but understanding heaves the air.
She turns away from what she knows he has to give.
Among these blunt Sofala hills, as winter light falls warm
bitterness chills her heart.

Delivery of mail is all that Blue, too old for war, can do to serve.
A sacred and a national duty.
An honour and a burden.
A postman's job is to deliver
no matter what.
Her family are his friends; her son a steady lad
who worked the goldfields hard
and laughed into the sober dawn of every day
and found war irresistible.

Deliver he must. Blue sits her softly down
beneath the branches of the cherry-plum
opens the envelope, unfolds the note, reads aloud.
His voice breaks.

She turns away and falls, surrendering
to earth's tricky stability
wanting to lie there with her son
tasting dirt and stones.
A crow laments. Trees weep.
It takes a year before she walks again.

The father makes enquiries:
His letter 'Army Records Officer: Dear Sir'
requesting details of the death
receives no answer.
The postman's job is to deliver the official story.
Their son was 'killed in action, May the fifteenth, 1917.'
They must be satisfied with that.

And yet…
Think of it as delicate and careful wisdom.
How can you tell a father that his son was blown to bits
among the mud and blood at Bullecourt?
A quick death, a kind death if you like
but better for the family not to know.
Better to leave them space to mourn
and dream him whole.

Currencies

This was my father:
a man taut-muscled, brown with surf and sun
a sportsman and a gentleman.
Enjoyed a drink, a smoke, a conversation.
Wove words like spells
winnowed gold coins from the hearts of stories
and scattered them all
over me.

This was myself:
a girl small-soft, unknown to darkness.
My family, home, my school, my friends
sang sweet.
The sun shone almost always.

The call to war was my father's boyhood dream come true.
The fight for God and King and country
the noblest duty of a man
his honour and his pride
a chance to prove yourself, to learn at last
if you had courage
enough.

I missed him; he was lost too long to battle
and to prison camps –
alive or dead: who knew?
I willed him light and life.

Came peace, so prayed for, lived for.
He survived, the family whole again.
His eyes were deep and hurt but warm with home.
This was a good man who had seen bad things.
The jungle railway grew inhuman fruit
and savage memories that stalked the night
and baulked at speech.
At home, with dignity he played the family role
winning the bread and cake as duty willed.
But only part of him returned
and never were there words past platitudes to share
never a way for us to talk of deeper truths
never a time for me to ask, and him to tell.
Gone were the stories and the laughter.
Our only common currency was love.

Travel Guide

Travel opportunities have been wide
and my menfolk made the most of them
at government expense
though, strictly speaking, nothing does come free.

Great-grandfather, a Sofala boy who rode his horse to
    Bathurst once,
caught the dawn boat to a Gallipoli beach.
The welcome was warm.
The accommodation not so hot.

Granddad loved the water, surfed
turned brown in Bondi sun
knew nothing of jungle
until a railway line was needed
which he and his companions built
through the Thai jungle for the Japanese.
Extras like cholera were provided.

My father planned to bushwalk in Tasmania
ended up in Vietnam instead.
The tropic experience was strangely ambivalent.
Friend might not be always so.
Honour was sometimes deemed dishonourable.
Rain, like words, could poison.

My brother learnt to ski at Perisher but
skiing was not offered in Afghanistan.
although a country set in mountains.
Walking tours were arranged.
You had to watch where you put your feet.

They all came home, my men, our men, with inward faces.
I pray my son grows up to travel less.

Tomorrow

Countdown

Accident on a mountain road:
B is the barricade, splitting and splintering at the
Corner too sharp for my turning.
D is for down as
Ecstatically into the sunset my car and I
Fly. Eagles soaring must feel like this. But remember
Gravity.
H is the hindsight that comes too late.
I should have loved 'slow' more.
J is the jolting at the base of the cliff.
K is the keening of my phone.
Let it ring till I reach it, please.
Movement is pain.
Now; I need that phone now
Otherwise – if I can't get to it, who will know I am here?
P is my phone, unreachable. Keep trying.
Q is the quality of despair.
Ringing…but
Silence too soon.
Tears.
U is the unknown closing in.
V is the value of a life. I
Wish with
Xcess of
Yearning to see the sun rise tomorrow…
Z is for zero. For nothingness. The end

of one thing,
the start of another when
Angels in helmets and yellow overalls
find me in the morning.

Just For Today

Just for today
above the sea the air is buoyant with persuasion
the cliff edge beckoning.

Just for today
to jump is not an act of cowardice or folly
but an affirmation of autonomy
a plea for self.

The cliff is sandstone. See its jewels of quartz
the layered creaminess, the veins of rust
the stories written here of changing seasons
eroded like the stories you yourself can tell:
the baby and the adult strong in trust
the broken man.
Fly here with birds all innocent of memory
and see below, so many memories away
deep water churning, spray attacking grim dark rocks.
See without fear.
The moments of your flight that stretch as far as thought
will never think of ending,
just for today.

But tomorrow, endings will be all.

I Am Emperor

I am Emperor of Planet Earth.
Mine is the power
above lesser creatures
to fly highest, move fastest
swim deepest.
Think thoughts, dream dreams
predict, create, analyse
theorise.
Craft philosophies
dare prophesies.
Destroy.

Earth tolerates my audacities
until they range too far, too high.
Alarmed by my capacities
she withers my crops, blows my cities away
eats up my villages with the fires of her belly.

I remember green forests
birds clotted in treetops
wheat gold in the sun
cities of glass
blue sky.
Once.

Now
I am Emperor of nothing.
Mine is the power
only to remember.

We Know That

…mountains are
something we can challenge
something we can stand on top of
and be higher than

…rocks are
resistant to press or push
intractable to change
like some of us

…earth is
a sure stability
on which we all are grounded
or like to think we are

but
when a mountain crumbles into rock
when a rock breaks up and crumbles into earth
when earth opens to swallow its own self
all certainties are vanquished
and what you see is not what you will get tomorrow.

How often will our tomorrows turn
to mock our yesterdays?

Only tomorrow knows.

Tomorrow We May Walk On Clouds

An idle thought
a push against accepted fact
that I open up the aircraft door
breathe in
step out…

   This much is certain
   that changes of speed and shape
   allow the plane to scuttle gravity
   skim plains, trees, mountains
   swoop over clouds.

…that I step out
to cloud banks
heaped like snow across blue air
ethereal fluffs
tempting as reassurance
luminous as faith.

   We thought we knew our world
   that seasons would come and go
   with decorum
   that governments would govern
   orderly.

   But now
   change visits us uninvited.
   Today it brings unwelcome gifts:
   old scars, new fears
   Mother Earth turned witch.
   Tomorrow?

After centuries, we learnt to fly.
Tomorrow
we may walk on clouds.

Endings

Quicksilver Girl

Hope is
dawn outlining buds on winter trees
a baby bird escaping shell, a hard seed shooting
a daughter's birth.
> *Hope was*
> *in the newborn's eyes opening to the world.*
> *The luminosity of all her days lit up our lives.*
> *A chosen one.*
> *Quicksilver girl.*

Hope is a rock slippery on ice.

Precision is
the order of the universe
the living crust of Earth.
> *Precision was*
> *the planet of her face*
> *the features sculpted kindly*
> *untidy curls a hint of anarchy.*
> *'I will climb that tree!'*

Precision is my chart of memories.

Certainty is
the sun rising each day. A fiery braggart, sure
but generous
its gift to Earth the fretful mystery of life.
   Certainty was
   the small girl waking.
   For her, time flowed, and every cent of it she used.
   Got value for it too, in full.
   'I want to go…' 'to see…' 'to be…
   She showed us that impossible was not a word.
   So little time…
   Somehow she knew.
   'I can do it,' she said, and did.
   Up to a point.
Certainty is my love for her
as unequivocal as grief
stranger than life
stronger than death.

One Dove

They throw petals from the headland
and let doves fly
remembering Bali. Grieving so
but I
see one dove only
turning in a distant sky.

One dove.
I watch you still in flight.
Quicksilver miss
open as sunshine
changeable as clouds
trusting as love.
I see you turning
pinned against the blue
and falling
sliding through green days and laughter
leaf flicker and fading light
into night.

One dove
flies my grief through a lonely sky.

Desert Song

The desert dunes shift as spirit voices sift
through sand and vacancy
calling to the traveller from the greens of known country
promising the traveller something more than the soft places
where rains and rivers play.

Not your fault if you turn from abundance
to walk into places empty of all but answers
as voices flute from the desert
singing the songs of sirens.
Not your fault if you are devoured by desert hyenas
who imitate the silver voices of seductresses
and you end as bones bleached by the light and heat.

You had to do it.
Did you find what you sought?

The Old Cemetery

The graves, tight-fisted guardians of the dead,
themselves are dying now
headstones fallen
names, epitaphs erased by time.

A slew of years has passed
since the exiles who called England 'home'
were buried here in a land that needed
learning
before it could be loved.
They learnt much
loved a little
still yearned for pale skies
and soft-leaved English gardens.
At the end, to rest them easy among strangeness
their graves were sown with memories.

Seeds swelled
sprouted
flowered, multiplied
and now

in early spring the snowdrops spike the grass
demurely
joined by freesias marking territory
with fragrance.
Wattle moves in, asserts its native rights
with a blaze of gold
then, season done, backs off
to summer roses neat, well-bred and sniffy
who know they are upper-class but
in time give way to coreopsis
the migrant from America
who, with a backward nod to wattle
spins bright across the graves.

And so, in every season in this space
natives and migrants weave hands through willing soil
and the company of the dead
cradles the new seeds' quickening.

The Butterfly in the Room

A living room.
Side tables. Chairs.
Books. TV.
Trinkets, pictures.
Brown wood.
Dust.

A room silent
as an unplayed violin.
Armchairs empty.
Books unthumbed.
Fine china gold rimmed
(kept for Occasions)
locked in cabinets
key lost.
Family photographs –
anonymity
with matching smiles.

A room of stories that could spill
a bean or three:
of angels offered tea and biscuits
devils booted out the door
suns risen, moon shine
tears shed, laughter
tangles untangled
dross turned to gold.

A room whose use-by-date
is passed
its vital heart extinguished
the treasures to be sold
the stories forgotten
because the children are young
and greedy for tomorrow
while the parents were old and have gone.
Dead dreams, their belongings now.

But in the old people's living
the quiet ripple of butterfly wings
changed the world.

'The Butterfly Effect' describes how small acts in one place can cause big changes in another. The name comes from the example that the flapping of a butterfly's wings in France could cause a hurricane in China.

One Moment Longer

Consider us, this paradox of opposites
called human.
Our songs vibrate through rainbow, ash
laughter and lament,
our movements flow shifty as desert dunes.
We speed, slow down
hear distant, near
see microscopic, telescopic.

The brain a storehouse of memory
impulses cruel, kind
betrayals, truths
guilt, innocence
greed, sacrifice.

Though locked in the world's confusions
the taking, the giving
the discontent of choice
we summon angels to stare the devils down
as we watch our loved ones die
wanting them, for just one moment longer
to touch the power
the utter urgency
of living.

Who'd Want?

Let me live with generosity
die with grace
happy to have been here
but ready to go
for who wants to live forever?

www.ingramcontent.com/pod-product-compliance
Lightning Source LLC
Chambersburg PA
CBHW071021080526
44587CB00015B/2450